5-MINUTE DRILL

A Simple Prewriting Process for Creating College-Level Essays

by Rich Mayorga, Ed.S.

SHERPALEARNING
GUIDING YOU TO EVEN GREATER HEIGHTS

Sherpa Learning is dedicated to helping high-achieving learners gain access to high-quality, skills-based instruction that is created, reviewed, and tested by teachers. To learn more about Sherpa Learning and our vision, or to learn about some of our upcoming projects, please visit us at **www.sherpalearning.com**.

Publisher/Editor: David Nazarian

Copy Editor: Christine DeFranco

Proofreader: Kristyna Zaharek

Cover Design: David Nazarian

Cover Image: © Syda Productions | Dreamstime.com

* AP is a registered trademark of the College Board, which was not involved in the production of, and does not endorse this product.

ISBN 978-1-948641-17-3

SHERPALEARNING
GUIDING YOU TO EVEN GREATER HEIGHTS

Printed in the United States of America.

10 9 8 7 6 5 4 3 2

This book is dedicated to all my students out there—past, present, and future. Thanks for sharing your lives with me. May your future be full of laughs (with or without puns), learning, and successes. Thank you, God bless, and be the best that you can be. Enjoy life!

Table of Contents

Introduction

The 5-Minute Drill is a wonderfully simple process designed to improve your writing skills. In the simplest terms, the 5-Minute Drill is a pre-writing system—a process to plan and write quality essays. It's similar to a rough outline, but because it's a self-generated graphic organizer, you won't be beginning with a blank page, as you would with an outline. Just quickly draw a couple of vertical lines on a blank piece of paper (no handouts required!), and you're ready to start filling in what you know. The 5-Minute Drill is comprised of specific segments that help guide you through the thinking process required for writing strong analytical and argumentative essays. After a short while, you will be writing highly-organized, high-quality essays.

It Works!

Students who have learned the 5-Minute Drill over the years, almost exclusively say they use the 5-Minute Drill's concepts in college classes and that it has dramatically enhanced their college experience. An almost-30-year-old former student of mine working in medical software design recently articulated his continued use of the 5-Minute Drill to me, along with a few small modifications to align it to his professional field. Another graduate from 2000 told me she used the 5-Minute Drill to successfully compose her doctoral dissertation (she used each 5MD paragraph indentation as a chapter). Virtually all my past students tell me they use the 5-Minute Drill in college and that it has greatly assisted their educational paths.

Improving your writing skills can be made more manageable with the 5-Minute Drill. To be clear, the more a writer can be guided organizationally and with answer-driven directives, the more his or her writing is enhanced. The principal difference from writing in the average high school setting to college-level writing is the application of causal relationships. The true answers in adult life are rarely isolated and simple; instead, the answers that ring the truest are answers that show the causes, effects, connections, and complexities of one's thesis to answer the question posed. The 5-Minute Drill is the precursory step to achieving college-level writing and thinking skills.

How It Works

The 5-Minute Drill will visually show you what needs to be done to write a complete essay. Every worthwhile essay rubric requires a solid thesis, reasonable topics, evidence, cause/effect relationships, transition sentences, flow, concrete mechanics, as well as a clear and complete answer to the question. The 5-Minute Drill assists this process visually, structurally, cognitively, and in a jigsaw-puzzle fashion that makes it easier and quicker to create a well-organized essay.

Virtually everyone can improve their writing skills, especially with some strategic pre-planning. When someone knows the content to answer a question, the process is simply the organization of information, writing mechanics, and "finishing" words. The 5-Minute Drill guides this process.

Consider these foundational skills for the writing of strong argumentative essays:

- The thesis should have a clear direction that answers the question.

- Each of the three body paragraphs should include a broad topic sentence.

- The body paragraph/specifics column should contain specific evidence that answers the question, which leads to the cause/effect answer.

- The goal should be answering the question while including the strongest evidence (by way of cause/effect) that one can muster.

- Quality transitions between the evidence and answer create flow and a sense of sophistication necessary for earning the highest rubric points.

- The essay's conclusion should summarize the key components to the question, through the stated thesis, connecting them with cause/effect relationships.

- The conclusion should clearly answer the thesis.

The graphic structure of the 5-Minute Drill promotes visual verification of all these skills, and will help you make connections between individual concepts and elements. Now you're not just writing scattered ideas in an essay hoping that some of them hit the target; instead, the 5-Minute Drill guides you directly toward that target, ensuring you end with a coherent, well-organized essay. Plus, it'll save you time!

Why It Works

Often in an attempt to write an essay, we provide plenty of specific evidence, but we forget to summarize how it all fits together – in short, we don't answer the question well. The 5-Minute Drill graphically verifies the essay's success and completion. It helps you get to the core of the answer—the causes and effects—allowing you to answer the question more efficiently and consistently write quality cause-and-effect-driven essays with less work and in less time!

The chief knock against the 5-Minute Drill is that some people perceive it as a formula-driven essay that limits creativity. To a minor degree, this may be true. Consider, though, that most of us learned the alphabet via repetition due to its consistent format; the same goes with the 5-Minute Drill. It is simply a pre-writing system to learn the process. Once it is well-practiced and deeply instilled, it can often be flexibly applied, whether it's on paper or through mental organization. Many of my past students that are now in college regularly report this fact to me—they may not write the process out on paper every time, but they do naturally draw it out in their heads. They can do this because they know the process so well.

This is another strength of the 5-Minute Drill: its flexibility. Anyone that utilizes the 5-Minute Drill can restructure or modify the system to better fit his or her needs. For example, the 5MD can accommodate different essay types, such as comparison-contrast, change-over-time, document-based questions, or any other type of standard essay question. If necessary, the 5-Minute Drill is flexible enough to make space for more requirements of the prompt: adding more body paragraphs, splitting the specifics column into two columns for different time periods or divided concepts, throwing in a contextualization paragraph, adding a literature-based component, including a document enhancement paragraph, or anything else that supplements your needs in order to answer the question. With simple modifications, the 5-Minute Drill can support virtually any writing task.

Worth Noting

The 5-Minute Drill takes some time to learn; most high school students pick it up after just a few attempts, plus some instructor sampling. The first handful of solo attempts often take 20 minutes or more to complete, but improvement comes with rehearsal. Practicing this system in small groups greatly assists the learning process. Each year my students go from a slow and awkward 5-Minute Drill at the beginning of the year to a quick (takes less than five minutes), quality drill by the final semester. The improvement of writing skills takes perseverance and practice, just like learning to ride a bike. The 5-Minute Drill may take you some time to master, but it will be worth it!

Introduction

The 5-Minute Drill helps writers get to the core of the answer, but the transition from the 5-Minute Drill to the actual essay does require reasonable essay-writing skills. Having a game plan like the 5-Minute Drill is far better than just throwing thoughts at a target, hoping that some ideas hit the correct mark, as many students are accustomed to doing. Yet even with a game plan, writing strong essays takes time and practice.

CHAPTER 1

Getting Started

A visual sample of a 5-Minute Drill will best prepare your mind to understand its simplicity and gain an overview of its functioning pieces. This is the core of the 5MD's graphic organizing. The design of this graphic organizer is at the core of this simple, yet highly effective approach to succinct, successful essay writing.

So grab a sheet of paper and, leaving space for a thesis statement at the top of the paper, place two vertical slashes on it. Now the thinking process begins! Please note the shape and spacing of the sample; the reasons for this spacing will be explained in detail later. The general format is included on the next page.

Thesis: key words of the question + era/years/setting + action verb
+ make a claim

Topics	**Specifics** (details/proper nouns/dates/data/info)	**Cause/Effect**

Conclusion: key words of the thesis + the cause/effect column's summary
= answers the thesis

CHAPTER 2

Writing a Strong Thesis

You've heard this before but it bears repeating: the most important sentence in any essay is the thesis. It should contain a time-frame or setting, the keywords of the question, an action verb, and a claim (although many variations can be used). In order to craft an effective thesis statement in this format, it helps to think of your thesis statement within the context of your introductory (or opening) paragraph.

The introductory paragraph of the 5-Minute Drill essay has a basic foundation of three or four sentences. The first sentence is a broad sentence that narrows the concept of the prompt into a manageable theme. The next sentence or two should establish the direction that will be taken to answer the question. Last, a clear, succinct thesis should be stated. Let's take a closer look using some examples.

First, read the prompts that follow. Example A, marked with the Uncle Sam icon, is a U.S. History prompt, and Example B, with the globe icon, is a World History prompt. We'll revisit these prompts as we progress through the steps of the 5MD. Completed 5MDs for both of the samples are provided in Chapter 7 (pages 42–47).

Example A

Prompt: *The global economy depends on U.S. interaction. Explain this statement by sharing a world region, with its specifics, to prove U.S. influences.*

 Example B

Prompt: *The Soviet Union had major impacts on world dynamics and history. Why was the Soviet Union created?*

Sentence 1 – Narrow the Focus

The broad, first sentence usually takes the prompt from a global question and shapes it into a manageable concept.

 Example A

The prompt is about one aspect of the global economy, so a quality first sentence may narrow it to the Pacific Rim's finances.

Example B

> The prompt deals with the former Soviet Union's impetus, so a narrowing direction may be to bring communist ideology into the first sentence.

Students often say they get "stuck" when writing the first sentence. Its creation can be stress-free if you use this simple process. The first sentence of the essay does not need to be something lengthy, dramatic, or flowery; it just needs to point the question in a manageable direction.

Sentence 2 – Establish Direction

The middle sentence or sentences of the first paragraph should begin to answer the question with the key direction (or directions) of the answer.

 Example A

> Stating "The U.S. is a Pacific Rim financial leader of technology that is currently being challenged by China" is an excellent start to a superior essay, both organizationally and conceptually.

Example B

Explaining "Communist ideology through the works of Karl Marx and its varied implementation via Lenin" would cover much ground in setting up the answer to the question.

The middle sentence in an introductory paragraph provides clear direction to the essay.

Sentence 3 – Answer the Question (The Thesis)

The final sentence of the introductory paragraph is *usually* the thesis itself. Using the keywords of the question in the thesis will assist with it clearly answering the question and ensuring that the thesis hits the heart of the question. This cannot be overstated—**use the keywords of the question in the thesis.** Framing the question's era or timeframe into the thesis assists in developing a clear answer. Including an action verb (not *is, was,* or *were*) in the thesis exponentially increases the essay's level of sophistication; this will best bring the thesis to life. Examples of illustrative words may be: *trigger, decimate, produce, impassion, decapitate, embody, mold, create, grind, enflame, empower, gravitate, build, divide, resulting in,* etc. Finally, there needs to be a solid claim to answer the question.

KEYWORD(S) OF THE QUESTION + ERA/YEARS/SETTING
+ ACTION VERB + MAKE A CLAIM

 Example A

Prompt: The global economy depends on U.S. interaction. Explain this statement by sharing a world region, with its specifics, to prove U.S. influences.

Sample Thesis: "The twenty-first-century Pacific Rim economy illustrates the competitive nature between the U.S. and its challengers in a high tech arena."

Keyword: economy

Era/Years/Setting: 21st century

Action Verb: illustrates

Claim: competitive nature of interactions

Example B

Prompt: The Soviet Union had major impacts on world dynamics and history. Why was the Soviet Union created?

Sample Thesis: "For most of the 20th Century, the Soviet Union's political ideology shaped the world's political landscape through aggression and totalitarianism."

Keyword: world

Era/Years/Setting: 20th century

Action Verb: shaped

Claim: aggression and totalitarianism

The action verbs for these two samples—*illustrates* and *shaped*—empower and drive these thesis statements.

Significant energy should be used to draft a quality thesis sentence. Reshape when needed—as many times as needed. This may happen to some degree as the specifics of the 5-Minute Drill are pieced together like a jigsaw puzzle to answer the prompt. While just starting out with the 5MD, it's a good idea to give yourself plenty of extra space at the top of your page to annotate and revise your thesis.

Keep in mind the 5-Minute Drill is just intended to be a quick sketch of the organization of the essay's major concepts; consequently, the first two sentences of the introductory paragraph may or may not be written into the 5MD. Sometimes just a word or two is all that's needed to help shape the mental direction of the essay.

The introductory paragraph sets the tone and direction for the rest of the paper—be brief, clear, and answer the question. Be aware, though, that the basic components of this approach to an essay are not written in stone. Utilizing this 3-sentence introductory paragraph format is a great *initial* step, but when confident, you can advance to a bit more sophisticated approach. Like most skills, writing is hierarchical. Nevertheless, having a basic system like the 5-Minute Drill means you'll never get "stuck."

CHAPTER 3

Moving from Thesis to Topics

Once the thesis is generally formulated (although it can be somewhat incomplete at this point), three topics should then be placed into the graphic organizer's first column—the topics column. Each of these three topics represents the key concept of their respective paragraphs, assuming your intent is to create a full 5-paragraph essay (the 5MD is flexible—create what the prompt leads you to do; four body paragraphs is fine, if needed). The topics should be broad strokes to the answer. For example, if the question is about the cause of a specific war, quality topics may include "greed," "geographical domination," "leadership," "scarcity," "religious domination," "pride," "vengeance," "political ideology," "elitism," "cultural unrest," etc. Be sure to keep topics broad and free of proper nouns. Each paragraph's topic is a quick view of the entire paragraph's concept. Let's return to the two examples.

 Example A

Prompt: *The global economy depends on U.S. interaction. Explain this statement by sharing a world region, with its specifics, to prove U.S. influences.*

Sample Thesis: "The twenty-first-century Pacific Rim economy illustrates the competitive nature between the U.S. and its challengers in a high tech arena."

Sample Topics: tech growth, economic gain, intellect

 Example B

Prompt: *The Soviet Union had major impacts on world dynamics and history. Why was the Soviet Union created?*

Sample Thesis: "For most of the 20th Century, the Soviet Union's political ideology shaped the world's political landscape through aggression and totalitarianism."

Sample Topics: populist upheaval, ideology, political landscape

Remember, the intent is to keep the 5-Minute Drill a quick and concept-driven organizational tool. The use of abbreviations is a useful skill, as long as it can be understood by the author (and the one who is grading/reviewing your 5-Minute Drill exercises, if applicable). Keeping each topic to as few words as possible is best. Placing more than two or three words into the topics column for a single paragraph is satisfactory, if needed, but be sure the lengthier wording is truly needed.

Also, to write the best essay possible, do not use proper nouns or specifics in the topics column. For example, if you are writing about the U.S. Government, do not use the three branches of government (Judicial, Legislative, Executive) as the three topics. Instead, use the *concepts* that the three branches represent as the topics (judging, laws & money, and leadership). Having broad paragraph topics that narrow to the evidence and cause/effect strengthens an essay through clarity of organization and conceptual development.

The Shoe Game

To help understand the creation of topics, my classes often use what I call *The Shoe Game*. This "game" will help you to see that you already know the answers; it's all about extracting the appropriate concepts for the appropriate space.

Here's the game: willing people put one of their shoes in the center of a circle of people. Once there are multiple shoes in the center of the classroom, list as many similarities and differences between the shoes as you can. For example, they all are used for feet, they all have soles, some have laces and some don't, they are different colors, they all cost money, etc. Next, divide the shoes up into *conceptual* groupings, keeping the groups as even as possible. Groups may include the shoes' purpose, weight, brand name, height, color, manufacturer, size, cushion, shape, etc. This is the same grouping skill needed to make the paragraph topics! If you can understand the shoe game, you can create topics for body paragraphs.

Remember that you know the general answers/topics; they are frequently repeated in the course lectures and are most often subtopics of the classroom texts. Use the topics that **best** answer the prompt, even if it takes you a few attempts. This is how you create a high-scoring response that fully answers the question.

P.E.R.S.I.A.

You may have already learned about the use of the acronym **P.E.R.S.I.A.** (P = political, E = economic, R = religion, S = social or cultural, I = intellectual, and A = arts). For basic history courses, the tendency is strong to use the standard political, economic, and social topics. These often lead to adequate answers, especially for broad, global-type questions.

As your writing's sophistication progresses, your topics can become more intricate. For example, a question may singularly encompass the "political" topic; so, the political theme should be broken down into three sub-topics—any combination of "political leadership," "political ideology," "political conflict," "political determinism," "socio-political dynamics," "political unrest," or "political ownership." Again, remember to use broad topics in the topics column to plan the most effective answer to the question.

With practice, you'll come to understand that the piecing together of topics is the beginning of the 5-Minute Drill's jigsaw-puzzle effect. This is a good approach to a well mapped-out essay. The process should not be difficult, but does require clear thinking in order to effectively connect concepts to support your thesis.

Continued use of the 5-Minute Drill will improve your ability to visualize the writing process with greater clarity. In time, you will find that the 5-Minute Drill compels you to analyze, synthesize, and evaluate, thereby improving your essay's sophistication.

CHAPTER 4

Using Specific
and Proper Nouns

O nce the topics have been established, it is best to then slide all the way over to the cause/effect column on the far right. Specifics added to the middle column now are likely to _not_ support your future answer, wasting time and effort. One must know the starting point _and_ endpoint of a "journey" to most efficiently travel to its successful completion. Nevertheless, to be lineal, let's take a look at the specifics column now before we get to the cause/effect column.

The middle column of the 5-Minute Drill contains specific evidence to support the essay's thesis. The specifics column should primarily have proper nouns, dates, wars/conflicts, supporting documents, data, people, quotes, places, and even concepts. **The specific evidence in each body paragraph should connect to the thesis through the topics.**

At this point, it is important to note that truly understanding the material is mandatory to effectively construct a successful response to the prompt. There are many answers to every question, but some answers are just more convincing and display a deeper understanding of the issue. Memorizing information can be helpful, but knowing how to connect, apply, and synthesize evidence into a coherent answer is an invaluable skill. With the 5-Minute Drill, this cognitive process is clear and visual.

Proper nouns that are placed into the specifics column should directly connect to your answer to the question (your thesis) by way of that particular concept (the corresponding topic). In other words, the topic of each paragraph should be the overarching concept tying the specific evidence in that paragraph to the answer. Let's look at an example.

 Example A

Prompt: *The global economy depends on U.S. interaction. Explain this statement by sharing a world region, with its specifics, to prove U.S. influences.*

Sample Thesis: "The twenty-first-century Pacific Rim economy illustrates the competitive nature between the U.S. and its challengers in a high tech arena."

Topic (1 of 3): tech growth

Specifics:

- importing and exporting numbers from Pacific Rim countries
- major players in the tech industry (Bill Gates and Microsoft)
- major countries' efforts to achieve tech progress
- major tech products
- the sequential growth of tech industries

The number of items in the specifics column for each body paragraph is dependent upon the question. A rough estimate of three items is acceptable in most cases. **Just be sure to answer the question.** Utilizing in-depth, specific knowledge of a few items is traditionally better than a laundry list of facts. It is certainly better to use concepts that lack facts than not writing any evidence at all, but the more specific the proof (evidence), the more one enriches their argument. Of course, other factors come into play (organizing the specific content within paragraphs, the flow of the content within the paragraph, the wording, the transitions that connect the information, overall writing skills, etc.), but the more factual evidence one provides, the more powerful the argument appears.

By visually checking your 5-Minute Drill, you can be sure that you have included enough evidence for each topic. You can then organize the specifics to improve the clarity and flow of your response. In this way, the 5-Minute Drill allows you to see the internal workings of an essay. Successful placement of the pieces of an argument into the 5-Minute Drill will reveal a "visually obvious" answer, resulting in significantly improved organization and a well-thought-out response.

Working with Sources

For those who desire to include primary source documents into a 5-Minute Drill, the specifics column is where the documents should be inserted. They should be linked to the corresponding paragraph's topic to best answer the question. Most often the documents of Document-Based Questions (DBQs) are there to assist with the cognitive direction of the answer. In other words, the documents should help determine the direction of your response. Remember to include information *beyond* the documents to completely answer the question and to earn the maximum number of rubric points. The 5-Minute Drill will help you visually organize the documents into an integrated and coherent essay that answers the question with specific evidence.

It is true that the specific facts and details can be difficult to extract from memory, but the particulars of the specifics column are the essence of the answer to the question. The specifics column *proves* the answer to the question through multiple pieces of appropriate, *specific* information.

CHAPTER 5

Establishing a Cause and Effect Relationship

As stated before, attempting to complete the cause/ effect column directly after the topics column is best for optimal organization and flow. It helps avoid wasting time and effort writing down specifics that do not match the thesis and are therefore unusable. Here again we see the jigsaw puzzle effect of the 5-Minute Drill—the overriding principle is to write down the parts you know, and then the rest of the information naturally falls into place as the answer to the thesis is connected, bit by bit, into organized paragraphs.

For clarification purposes, the final column's title is "cause/ effect"—this is intended to embrace any cause *and/or* effect relationships that may answer the question. The purpose of having both names, *cause* and *effect*, is to keep all opportunities for causal relationships open.

Oftentimes, cause and effect can be very different perspectives of the same issue, while other times they may be similar. Either way, the goal is to use the most effective path to answer the question. That path may include information about how one thing led to, or caused, something to happen, or it may include information about how that same thing was effected by another thing. To get a better understanding, let's take another look at the Pacific Rim example.

 Example A

Prompt: *The global economy depends on U.S. interaction. Explain this statement by sharing a world region, with its specifics, to prove U.S. influences.*

Sample Thesis: "The twenty-first-century Pacific Rim economy illustrates the competitive nature between the U.S. and its challengers in a high tech arena."

Topic: tech growth

Cause/Effect: economic stimulation

So here, the writer is saying that technological growth leads to economic stimulation. However, the writer could have also have chosen to prove that tech growth was caused by entrepreneurial activities. Though these examples go in different directions, both are correct.

The ultimate goal of any worthwhile essay is to answer the question. The 5-Minute Drill will visually provide you with the clearest, most direct path to the essay's answer. If there is not enough inclusion of any individual segment of the essay, the 5-Minute Drill will graphically display the omission so the error can be corrected and the essay's core information become more directed to the answer. If the listed cause/effect has a weak connection to the thesis or the evidence, it can easily be detected.

You may find that there are times when you think your 5-Minute Drill is nearly finished but you realize that it makes sense to switch the topic and cause/effect. That's fine. The recommendation is to do what is best to answer the question. Let's revisit the Soviet example for a closer look.

 Example B

Prompt: *The Soviet Union had major impacts on world dynamics and history. Why was the Soviet Union created?*

Sample Thesis: "For most of the 20th Century, the Soviet Union's political ideology shaped the world's political landscape through aggression and totalitarianism."

Topic: populist upheaval

Cause/Effect: totalitarianism

If populist upheaval led to totalitarianism, then use populist upheaval as the topic and totalitarianism as the cause/effect, but if it works better switching the two concepts to answer the thesis, then use them that way. Think of these cause/effect concepts as "mini-answers" to the question. Use them wherever they best match your thinking while you answer the question.

To summarize, the cause/effect column is an open opportunity to apply **causal relationships** leading to or coming from a defined topic, as **proven** by clear and accurate specifics.

CHAPTER 6

Writing a Conclusion

A worthwhile conclusion summarizes the essay through the paper's stated cause/effect reasoning. Using the keywords and/or concepts of the thesis, added to the causal relationships, formulate an adequate conclusion. Each body paragraph should have a major cause/effect listed; these SUB-concepts should answer the question, especially when they are combined with the thesis to form a conclusion.

Customarily, an adequate conclusion is not a lengthy or complex paragraph. Often, the conclusion can be a single sentence. A concise conclusion that answers the question is all that is needed. Still, with some essays, there is a flow that needs to be explained; therefore, there are times some length works better (for example, change-over-time questions), but this is only for a minority of answers.

Additionally, do not bring up new thoughts in the conclusion. The conclusion is about connecting what's already been explained in the paper. The priority is to answer the thesis with cause/effect relationships in a clear and succinct manner.

Writing a Conclusion

 Example A

Prompt: *The global economy depends on U.S. interaction. Explain this statement by sharing a world region, with its specifics, to prove U.S. influences.*

Sample Thesis: "The twenty-first-century Pacific Rim economy illustrates the competitive nature between the US and its challengers in a high tech arena."

Sample Conclusion: "U.S. interaction and technological creativity has led to economic stimulation and power in the Pacific Rim. The U.S. may be the tech giant today, but is being challenged."

 Example B

Prompt: *The Soviet Union had major impacts on world dynamics and history. Why was the Soviet Union created?*

Sample Thesis: "For most of the 20th Century, the Soviet Union's political ideology shaped the world's political landscape through aggression and totalitarianism."

Sample Conclusion: "For much of the 20th Century, the Soviet Union's ideological and political landscape shaped the planet through its aggression and totalitarianism for its own gain."

Brief conclusions are commonplace—even expected—
in college-level writing. Traditionally, conclusions are
necessary, but they are usually not of massive importance to
a worthwhile essay. In fact, in a timed essay, if you were to
run out of time, excluding the conclusion would do the least
amount of rubric-scoring damage as compared to the thesis
or cause/effect relationships. What matters is that the essay
does a worthwhile job of answering the question.

Chapter 7

Putting It All Together

Learning the 5-Minute Drill is a lot like learning to ride a bike; it takes time and practice, and most people learn in sequential steps. Often some people learn the 5-Minute Drill quickly and some learn at a slower pace. Your pace is not important. Rather, the priority of this prewriting activity is understanding the writing concepts so you can better answer the question.

Before we start writing some samples, here are a few bits of experiential advice to help you easily and effectively learn to navigate the 5-Minute Drill. Some of these were mentioned along the way, but they're worth repeating.

Essential Tips

1. You do not need to write down the first two sentences of the introductory paragraph in your 5-Minute Drill during a timed esssay (unless the instructor requires it), as long as you know to place them in the final essay. If desired, jot down a few

words to help remember a concept. The 5-Minute Drill is just the basic thinking of an essay; moving along quickly and catching your thoughts before they escape your mind is a most crucial objective.

2. It is not a good idea to rewrite the question on another paper in a timed essay. Positioning the key words, era, and direction of the question into the thesis is the best way to ensure that all of the angles are covered and to effectively answer the question.

3. Leave some extra space at the top of the paper when writing the original thesis; it will often be redesigned as the jigsaw-puzzling of the graphic organizer happens naturally.

4. There will be times when your 5-Minute Drill is created in an unorderly fashion—the topics may be first or last, the specifics may pop into your mind in a random manner, you may decide to flip-flop a topic and cause/effect, or the process may yield heavier results in one paragraph's specifics column than another. All of these scenarios are fine because they are part of the jigsaw-puzzling process. Use the visual nature of the 5MD to assist you in piecing together a more coherent and worthwhile draft.

5. Make the specifics column most of the paper's width. The first and last columns (topics and cause/ effect) need only a small bit of space, but the middle (specifics) column will need more space to create

the opportunity for appropriate, dynamic, and clear evidence that will answer the question. This seemingly unimportant tidbit will pay dividends later.

6. Make the 5-Minute Drill's three rows (for each individual paragraph's information) as tall as possible. This is the easiest beginner's mistake to correct. If you leave only minimal space to write your specific information, it often negatively affects the answer because you've limited the essay's possibility for conceptual growth.

7. Abbreviate whenever possible when creating a 5MD, as long as you (and your instructor, if that be the case) can understand the meanings of your abbreviations later (e.g. "pol." for political, "ec." or "$" for economic, "soc." for social, "cap." for capitalism, "gov." for government, etc.). Six letters (two words abbreviated by three letters each) may produce the opportunity for two or three meaningful sentences in the actual essay. Other than Sample Drill G1 (page 46), little of this skill is demonstrated in this book; organizational clarity and understanding have been the foremost objective here.

8. Underlining a key concept (or concepts) in the specifics column—so you may further contextualize the concept(s) in the formal essay—may greatly assist with answering the question and, therefore, ensure you gain maximum rubric points.

Underlining takes no time at all, yet it is a valuable code to remind yourself of something for the final essay.

9. Writing a conclusion into your 5-Minute Drill is helpful while still learning the process, but as your writing skills mature, the conclusion is easily accomplished with little pre-writing. By the end of the school year in my classroom, conclusions are only required when they are necessitated by a unique arrangement of cause/effect relationships that strongly guide the answering of the thesis. In other words, by the end of the school year, my students write the conclusion with the 5-Minute Drill *only* when it's necessary to answer the question.

10. When just starting out with the 5-Minute Drill, you should expect to create several drafts for a single essay, assuming there is not a timed element to the activity. Early in the school year, my students are expected to write three drafts. Take time to create and reshape as many drafts as desired when getting to know the process of the 5-Minute Drill.

11. The 5-Minute Drill lends itself to quick organization, especially when it comes time to transfer the graphic organizer's information into a full, five-paragraph essay. One way to improve this process is to evaluate the 5-Minute Drill's topics to decide which should go first, second, and last in the essay. Your style will come into play here—while one writer may lead off with the strongest argument, other writers

save the best argument for last. Whichever way it works out, just ensure that the argument is logical and sequential. Do this by jotting down a quick "1," "2," and "3" for each topic. Then number the items for each paragraph in the specifics column. This organization can improve your essay's clarity and assist the effort to answer the question.

12. While still learning the process of the 5-Minute Drill, it is recommended to write out all of the pieces. As the school year moves along, you can write fewer and fewer words without losing the concepts and meanings. Next, you can abbreviate more and more, as long as the abbreviations are obvious. More than just a savings of time, the rapid flow of information facilitates your ability to integrate course content into your answer. In other words, working quickly can help your brain recall more specific information, leading to a stronger response. The "5-Minute" part of the 5-Minute Drill is more than just a benefit of the process; it is a part of the prewriting process.

13. It is important to note that not everyone can *easily* move from a completed 5MD to a full essay. Begin by shaping your 5-Mintue Drill's concepts into sentences, like you would use in everyday conversation with your friends. Keep your thesis in mind so you always move toward answering the question. If you find that you're struggling with the transition, there are two things you can do to improve this. First, practice! Use the samples provided in this book to strengthen your ability

to transition from a 5MD to an essay. **Effort equals product!** If needed, tutoring from peers or instructors can be a major help.

Sample Drills

A finished example of a preliminary, how-to-learn prompt and a 5-Minute Drill is presented here:

Question A *Quality writing skills will benefit your career and life. Explain.*

Thesis: Quality academic skills, especially writing, will prepare me for college, boost my academic performance, take me to higher level occupations, and improve my standard of living.*

Topics	Specifics	Cause/Effect
• acad. skills	• competition w/ other students = opportunities • 5-Minute Drill = success/knowledge/power • thinking skills = acad. skills = achievement • Ruby Scholarship	• acad. achievement
• acad. performance	• knowing "Drive Time" software = job • better education = my 1st job & better job • Professor "Z" modeling • physics class story of writing success = top job	• better job

Topics	Specifics	Cause/Effect
• improved prep.	• improved maturity, use class data • superior thinking skills = better decisions • standard of living will improve via better jobs • higher income level = happier • 2016 college choice story = better life	• better life

Conclusion: Quality academic skills, especially writing, will prepare me for college through more academic achievements to earn the employment and lifestyle that benefits my life.

* Note that the more competent thesis statements won't just cite the topics. It may be more beneficial to lead the reader with more enticing syntax. The first sentence or two of the introductory paragraph will assist with this flow and sophistication.

Question B: *For years this class has been the subject of criticism due to its excessive homework load. Evaluate how this classroom views this situation in the short and long term.*

Thesis: Homework requires discipline which creates opportunities for students to succeed at this level and the next. Opportunities come to those who are willing to work hard for their future successes.

Topics	Specifics	Cause/Effect
• h/w quantity	• not all classes have homework = AP has more • 4 hours h/w per week will help me later • Improved discipline skills lessens homework load • practice improves it all = discipline	• discipline
• h/w quality	• homework is thinking skills, not busy work • vocab growth helps every angle of life • h/w = knowledge = power • planning & habits will help now & later	• thinking skills

Topics	Specifics	Cause/Effect
• motivation	• effort = product • instructor's sample stories of success... 1st job • h/w is quality for my career path • achieves my purposes (now and career)	• successes

Conclusion: Homework discipline will create opportunities; for example: thinking skills for students to succeed at this level and for a lifetime career.

Question C: *High school students can improve their standardized test scores with appropriate choices. Explain, with specifics, outcomes of this philosophy.*

Thesis: Goals to attain exemplary standardized test scores improve high school students' opportunities for more college scholarships, lead to a better education and solid career paths.

Topics	Specifics	Cause/Effect
• abilities	• good educational practices = more skills • practicing reading/writing/math skills = test success • practice tests lead to higher scores • tests = competition for scores/scholarships	• more scholarships
• motivation	• hard work = higher stand. test scores • effort = product • 8 hours of homework per week = better learning • Peer efforts help encourage me	• better education

Topics	Specifics	Cause/Effect
• desire	• my inspiration = X career field • not fall prey to teenage temptations • parents encourage me regularly • higher than a "NN" score on my SAT = my goal	• more career opportunities

Conclusion: To ultimately create the career opportunities high school students desire, higher standardized test scores assist in earning more scholarships while improving the level of education for motivated and skilled students.

Writing a **compare and contrast** answer is especially easy with the 5-Minute Drill; there are two ways to handle the formatting. The shortest mode is to make one topic "similarities," the second paragraph "differences," and the third paragraph, whatever is the question's theme. The other way is simply to split the second column (specifics column) in half, vertically (See Question D below). This will again provide visual verification of successfully contrasting the other angle. This style of 5-Minute Drill is a bit more challenging to transfer to a 5-paragraph essay format. As such, it may take a bit of practice but often produces a more sophisticated answer. The 5-Minute Drill formatting is an excellent, graphic visual of an organized answer. An example is provided below:

Question D: *Compare and contrast the 5-Minute Drill to other pre-writing activities with successes and weaknesses.*

Thesis: The 5-Minute Drill is a complete pre-writing activity in comparison to other types of pre-writing tools due to its graphic design characteristics, which leads to review capabilities, as well as being an outstanding diagnostic tool.

Topics	Specifics of 5MD	Specifics of Others	Cause/ Effect
• student's view	• Visual jigsaw growth • View to systematically build answer • Standardized tool • Complete outlook • Visual representation	• webbing = messy • just scattered words • myriad of types • only pieces	• graphic jigsaw puzzle "building"
• classroom system	• Forces use of specifics • Empowers writers = students "see" concepts • Re-applies class material • Pushes cause/effect	• Not a complete writing package = not review style for a classroom • Lacks cause/effect connections	• review tool
• visual diagnostics	• thesis • topics • specifics • cause/effect • conclusion	• pieces of writing • lacks growth & connectedness to the thesis • does not push cause/effect	• improves writing

Conclusion: The 5-Minute Drill is a complete pre-writing activity in comparison to other types of pre-writing tools because of how it improves students' writing skills through its visual growth of conceptual answers, its in-class review application, and pushing the use of cause/effect dynamics to answer the question well and completely.

Question E: *The 13 American colonies developed into unique cultural and economic regions by 1740. Explain.*

Thesis: Culture and economics created separate and unique environments in each of the three regions of the 13 American colonies by 1740.

Topics	Specifics	Cause/Effect
• industry	• New England: Mass., N.H., R.I., Conn. • industry: shipbuilding, lumbering, fishing • primarily Puritans (later Congregationalists) • education promoted • salutary neglect often used • birthplace of Great Awakening	• powerful economic and religious leadership

Topics	Specifics	Cause/Effect
• breadbasket	• Middle Colonies: Del., N.Y., N.J., Penn. • Wheat + = main food producer of colonies • Anglican Church – more connected to Britain = similar in farming, too • huge change due to the Great Awakening • Quakers were a major direction/force - pro-peace, anti-slavery, crimeless • salutary neglect often used	• productive British colonies
• plantations	• Southern Col: Maryland, Virg., Geo., N & S Car • plantations – slavery, rice, & indigo boomed • Anglican Church – more connected to Britain • cultural stratification promoted • nearer to Spanish Florida	• "distant" colonies for slavery

Conclusion: By 1740, the 13 American colonies had developed into 3 distinct regions due to issues of economics through slavery and religion.

Question F: *The global economy depends on U.S. interaction. Explain this statement by sharing a world region, with its specifics, to prove U.S. influences.*

Thesis: The twenty-first-century Pacific Rim economy illustrates the competitive nature between the U.S. and its challengers in a high tech arena.

Topics	Specifics	Cause/Effect
• tech growth	• import & export #s (specifically) • tech. leaders lead the world (Bill Gates) • US efforts = #1 in tech output (via Eng. language) • resources = sequential US tech. growth (globalization is modifying this concept daily)	• economic stimulation
• economic gain	• money makes US the leader • US culture values $ more, traditionally (Japan gains) • $ = political gain = military gain = power • US = #1 exporter in Pacific Rim, China challenging	• economic power

Topics	Specifics	Cause/Effect
• intellect	• US = hotbed of ingenuity (Steve Jobs) • US tech companies reign (Microsoft, Apple, etc.) • 3/7 of world pop. own cell phones = US lead • tech. stratification promotes more ideas	• creativity

Conclusion: U.S. interaction and tech. creativity has led to economic stimulation and power in the Pacific Rim. The U.S. may be the tech giant today, but is being challenged.

Putting It All Together

Question G: *The Soviet Union had major impacts on world dynamics and history. Why was the Soviet Union created?*

Thesis: For most of the 20th Century, the Soviet Union's political ideology shaped the world's political landscape through aggression and totalitarianism.

Topics	Specifics	Cause/Effect
• populist upheaval	• 1917 Bolshevik Revolution = upheaval • death of Czar/Russia • Marx's Communist Manifesto = words only • Russians hard-pressed into struggling USSR • Communist Party (top 1%) ruled	• totalitarianism
• ideology	• oligarchy controlled USSR • new Soviet traditions created (1917-1991) • attempts to gain Asian/European lands for Comm. • plutocracy = $ = military gain = political power	• political aggression

Topics	Specifics	Cause/Effect
• political landscape	• Marxist policies…..Politburo & Premier • totalitarian regime = Communism • Ruble = currency of USSR only = $ pol. domination • benefitted from the Cold War (anti-USA) • ideology = impetus for growth/ pol. direction	• political gain

Conclusion: For much of the 20th Century, the Soviet Union's ideological and political landscape shaped the planet through its aggression and totalitarianism for its own gain.

In an effort to provide an example of what a 5-Minute Drill will probably look like by the end of the school year, below is the same question (G) as above but it contains the abbreviated and shortened version of the same responses.

Question G1: *The Soviet Union had major impacts on world dynamics and history. Why was the Soviet Union created?*

Thesis: 20th Cent. USSR pol. ideology shaped W. pol. landscape via aggres./totalit.

Topics	Specifics	Cause/Effect
• populist upheaval	• Bolsh. Rev. = no Czar/Russia • Marx's Comm. Man. = words • Russians forced • Comm. Party = 1% rule	• totalit.
• ideology	• oligarchy = control • new Soviet (1917-91) • gain Asian/Eur. • $ = military = pol. pwr.	• pol. aggression

---

Topics	Specifics	Cause/Effect
• pol. landscape	• Politburo / Premier • Ruble = pwr. • Cold War benefits (anti-USA) • ideology = growth/pol.	• pol. gain

Conclusion: 20th Cent. Soviet's ideological/pol. landscape shaped… aggression / totalitarianism for its own gain

Sample Essays

Essay #1—by Jessie Salas, Sunnyside High School, Tucson, AZ

Question: *To what extent was the American Reconstruction Era successful?*

Thesis: The American Reconstruction Era 1865–1877 was only minimally successful; it did not completely integrate the South into the North—tangled by an inferior economy and grave social prejudice.

Topics	Specifics	Cause/Effect
• proposed reconstruction	• Lincoln's Ten Percent Plan • Radical Republicans, Reconciliationists, White Supremacists, Emancipationists • Lincoln vs. Johnson	• pleased few people
• reconstruction attempts	• Civil War Amendments • Black Codes • rise of White Supremacy • Andrew Johnson (veto) • carpetbaggers/scalawags • radical agendas of social groups	• assimilation virtually impossible

Topics	Specifics	Cause/Effect
• unsuccessful integration	• Black Codes • sharecropping system • Colfax Massacre • Cotton dependency = inferior economy • Panic of 1873 • Contrast between North/South	• South/North different

Conclusion: Reconstruction failed to fully reintegrate the South due to their differences.

Jessie Salas

April 10, 2018

After the American Civil War, there was a need to integrate the former Confederate States of America back into the Union, but conflicting factions had different ideas about how to effectively achieve this goal. What resulted was a limited integration of the American South into the North due to their many differences. The American Reconstruction Era 1865-1877 was only minimally successful; it did not completely integrate the South into the North - tangled by an inferior economy and grave social prejudice.

There were a number of factions in the United States who had proposed numerous ideas about how Southern Reconstruction should be handled, for example: Radical Republicans (those who wanted to punish the South for their indignities of war), reconciliationists, white supremacists, and emancipationists. The most significant idea however, was Abraham Lincoln's 10% Percent Plan, which would have allowed states in rebellion to rejoin the Union when 10% of their populations had taken an oath of allegiance to the United States. This probably would have allowed for the swift, political integration of the South into the North, but due to the assassination of Lincoln, this plan was never carried out, leading to the questionable integration headed by Andrew Johnson. Johnson's plan for Reconstruction would further the divide the North and South due to his opinion of blacks as "less" than that of Lincoln's Plan, allowing for less black social welfare/respect in the South as opposed to the North; hence blacks were often oppressed. Relatively speaking, white southerners were not pleased either. Although Reconstruction could not please everyone, it seemed to please very few people.

The Reconstruction Era was characterized by legislation and the rise of new groups of people in the United States. The most revolutionary pieces of legislation enacted during Reconstruction were the XIII, XIV, and XV Amendments which granted African-Americans emancipation,

Salas - 2 of 5

51

citizenship and suffrage; these however, would later be undermined by future southern Black Codes, which would render the amendments trivial. Groups such as the White Redeemers and the Ku Klux Klan rose to power during Reconstruction and helped to impede effective reintegration of the South, as well as lynching murdering many African-Americans. Another barrier to the successful reintegration was Andrew Johnson and the numerous vetoes he issued against congressional acts aimed to aid African-Americans. Carpetbaggers and scalawags were a large group of people who contributed to the struggles of the South. To contextualize, social groups added fuel to the fire of which would call for the unsuccessful reintegration of the South due to radical agendas. Whether it be racial discrimination or economic trial, social groups were primarily to blame for the multitude of problems faced by the South. Greed and emotion led to radical groups committing heinous acts against African-Americans, which split the morals of the North and the South even further apart. The pro-white opinions of the South would prove to conflict with the leftist views of the North, making total assimilation of both sides near impossible.

Reactions across the South would prove the somewhat unsuccessful nature of Reconstruction though radical expression. Black Codes back this hypothesis, as poll taxes and literacy tests limited many African-American's ability to vote in the American South. Black Codes also served to enslave blacks economically as they entered an economy that they could not properly perform in without skills or money. African-Americans were still being economically oppressed after the Civil War (e.g. tenant farming, sharecropping and crop-lien systems) despite a northern attempt to give them freedom. The Colfax Massacre is another piece of evidence that shows a divide between the North and South – an obvious attempt of whites to punish and murder any African-American attempt at equality. Adding to the differences of the South, the South could not compete economically with the North. An economy that relied almost entirely on cotton could not integrate well into an economy based on industry (the New South never truly emerged), especially after the Panic of 1873, which cut cotton prices in half, and therefore hurt the South's economy even more. These radical discrepancies in northern and the southern social and economic backgrounds rendered the Reconstruction of the South trivial. Although the era did produce a few great pieces of legislation, such as the Civil War Amendments and the Force Acts, the South was too opinionated to fully reintegrate with the North. The two sides were just too different.

The American Reconstruction Era 1865-1877 failed in fully reintegrating the South into the North because of their differences; both sides were dissatisfied. These differences of opinions on how to treat African-Americans kept assimilation between the two hemispheres virtually impossible. Radical groups, economic tendencies and pieces of legislation also pushed this divide further, along with radical reaction from the South. These differences allowed the South to only minimally integrate with the North.

Salas - 5 of 5

Essay #2 by Danissa Bojorquez, Sunnyside High School, Tucson, AZ

Question: *Explain why American consumerism changed so dramatically after WWII.*

Thesis: Post-WWII America spawned changes; economic expansion was dramatic. Consumerism after WWII mushroomed as product buyers increased their standard of living through economic expansion, giving way to buying newly developed products.

Topics	Specifics	Cause/Effect
• culture	• products – will help all • all sucked in • Dr. Spock • music & suburbs	• "need" for goods
• tech.	• TV – Kennedy/Nixon + entertainment • advertisement & media • suburbia: conformity, Levittown, + • credit cards	• consumerism increase

Topics	Specifics	Cause/Effect
• jobs	• GI Bill = education + loans • Cold War = jobs = STEM via arms race/Sputnik • Marshall Plan • jobs = $ to buy products = more jobs…	• standard of living & $ improvement

Conclusion: Consumerism provided "need" for new products, increased standard of living, and reshaped the US into an insatiable, consumer-driven economy.

Danissa Bojorquez

April 10, 2018

With the Second World War in the rearview mirror, America spawned rock n' roll, drive-ins, fast foods, "fast" families, credit cards and other changes; economic expansion was dramatic. Consumerism after WWII mushroomed as product buyers increased their standard of living through economic expansion, giving way to buying newly developed products.

The 1950s American culture was based on consumerism. Products they heard about just seemed to make life better and easier, additionally, these products were considered top technology for the day, from televisions to toasters. Every type of American, whether a beatnik (some of the few non-conformists of the era) or a conformist to society, was intrigued by these products. Mothers of the baby boom (1946-64) bought into the fashionable child-rearing lessons of Dr. Spock's book

Bojorquez - 1 of 5

on how to raise children with leniency, permitting a new youth culture to grow. The baby boomers developed a fever for "new" music of 'rock and roll,' fast food like McDonalds, Disneyland, suburbia, fast cars and drive-ins – products and services that developed only after the world war due to the American "need" for more and better goods.

Virtually every American home had a television by the end of the 1950s, and if that were not the case there were a couple of neighborhood friends that did. On television, young Kennedy's election against famous red-hunter Nixon had been witnessed, as well as advertisements based on new consumer products for the home, children's toys and much more. Advertisements prominently shaped American consumer desires. The media played a grand role in consumerism of the age whether you bought into politics or entertainment. Politicians sometimes bought the votes of viewers through heavy hearted stories to induce sympathy for the candidate. Entertainment, on the other hand, captured the life in a seemingly perfect suburban home depicting the perfectly dependent wife tending to her nuclear family. The majority of American adults were sold into the idea of living in suburbia, the perfect atmosphere of conformity to raise a family, as seen on television. To contextualize, Levittowns blossomed; methods used in war were the same methods used in constructing suburban homes in so-called "track houses" complete with a white picket fence and 2.5 children. Suburban life often began with moving to "cities outside the cities," as well as to the Sunbelt, as migration led people to the West and South since technology had made life in ultra-hot climates livable. Suburban life with the technology of the day became common in a baby-boom American culture of the 1950's, much because it was relatively easy to buy a home due to the credit system and credit cards of the day. Credit cards gave way to more accessibility to products; this available and fluid credit made growing consumerism become the norm of post-WWII America.

The end of the war worried many Americans of another depression, as troops

returned home needing jobs. The G.I. Bill
of Rights offered servicemen tuition
assistance for school and low interest
rates on government loans. This furthered
economic growth by boosting education
and consumerism. School tuitions helped
veterans go to college, study a profession,
then work in that particular field and earn
wages - wages then used to buy goods.
Employment in industry required special
skills, which often opened up occupations
for specialized work creating wages for
workers to later spend, even amid Cold
War tensions. The Marshall Plan assisted
Europe's post-war regeneration, while
consumerism drove the American economic
engine. Still, the Cold War threat felt
real; this led to an enhanced schooling
regime consisting of studies in mathematics
and science to counter the Soviet Sputnik
and the arms race. Americans furbished
their homes, and some, their bomb shelters.
More products led to more jobs; more jobs
led to more products in new homes to make
life easier and better with the new washing
machines, refrigerators, vacuum cleaners,
televisions, record players, and more - it

Bojorquez - 4 of 5

was the new American way. This burst of consumerism improved the American standard of living and greatly expanded the US economy.

Consumerism in America was dramatically altered after WWII, for it had demonstrated a new "need" for products, marketing, credit and opportunities that vastly reshaped Americans' minds and standard of living. Americans bought into a strong and seemingly insatiable, consumer-driven economy.

Putting It All Together

Appendices

Practice
Writing Prompts

For your assistance, a variety of practice writing prompts is provided below. There are two variations of each prompt, so you can choose the items that better fit your studies. Each set of prompts includes organizational hints for the 5-Minute Drill.

Question 1A: *Evaluate the impact Upton Sinclair's book,* The Jungle, *had on American society.*

Question 1B: *Evaluate the impact that the concepts behind Jared Diamond's book,* Guns, Germs, and Steel, *had on American society.*

This is an easy call for the three "standard" 5-Minute Drill history topics of political, economic and socio-cultural.

Question 2A: *What country is currently winning the space race? Why is there one leader and what effects will this have on future generations?*

Question 2B: *What country is currently winning the arms race? Why is there one leader and what effects will this have on future generations?*

Hopefully, it is recognizable that the three portions of this type of question will each garner their own respective paragraph in a 5 paragraph essay: (1) why/what creates space race leadership, (2) which country is winning the space race with its reasoning, and (3) the effects of this race.

Question 3A: *Explain the impact of the Nineteenth Amendment on the progression of women's rights in modern America.*

Question 3B: *Explain the impact of the English Bill of Rights on the progression of people's rights 1689 through 1783 in Europe and the new America.*

This type of essay can be driven, among other choices, by a change-over-time flow, or be broken into political, economic, and social/cultural paragraphs. The three paragraph topics for a change-over-time flow could be: the fight for suffrage, post-suffrage, and the modern American woman. There are many options to make this work.

Question 4A: *Compare and contrast views of US overseas imperialism in the late 19th and early 20th centuries. Share how American national identity of the time helped shape these views.*

Question 4B: *Compare and contrast views of Spanish overseas imperialism in the 16th and 17th centuries.*

It's quite easy and effective to write one topic "similarities/compare," the second topic "differences/contrasts," and the third topic be a theme to the question, for example, "imperialism" or "national identity" to clearly answer the question. Compare and contrast questions are quite simple to organize into 5-Minute Drills, although the specifics still need to answer the question well with cause/effects that connect to the theme of the thesis.

Question 5A: *Theodore Roosevelt reshaped the office of the US presidency. Provide evidence and effects of his political directions, efforts, and style.*

Question 5B: *Simon Bolivar reshaped South America. Provide evidence and effects of his political directions, efforts, and style.*

This should be easy to spot the organization for this prompt; the question clearly lists the three topics for you: "political directions, efforts and style". Note that the prompt asks to provide evidence and effects – these are already embedded in the 5-Minute Drill's structure. Again, this verifies some of the many attributes of the 5-Minute Drill.

Question 6A: *The 19ᵗʰ century US has responded differently to diverse international crises that have culminated in war. Explain.*

Question 6B: *The Roman Empire responded differently to diverse enemies throughout its reign. Explain.*

Be careful to keep the topics all common (not proper) nouns. It feels easy to list wars in the topics column, but this is not in the interest of achieving the best answer. Out of the many options for topics, some good ones may be: political ineptitude, economic demands, greed, land grabbing, despots, cultural imperialism, insurrection, cultural hatred, defensive repercussions, etc. Interestingly, some of these same thoughts may fit into the cause/effect column as well, depending on the direction the specifics properly defended.

Question 7A: *Indentured servants were often seen as middle class Americans of the 17ᵗʰ and 18ᵗʰ centuries. How can this be true?*

Question 7B: *Serfs of the Middle Ages are sometimes seen as the middle class of their era. Defend this statement.*

Because this unique concept is often not taught directly in history classes, you may need to ponder the direction of the answer a bit. Hence, specifics may need to be started before the topics for this question are realized. Piecing the answer together would lead one to create topics such as: economic stature, work ethics, societal hierarchy, cultural expectations, political opportunities, economic opportunities, technological opportunities, cultural demands, or desire for success. Any of these could work well and easily be supported with quality specifics and thematic cause/effects. Be sure to answer the question: true or not?

Question 8A: *Illustrate the extent of the importance of the US Constitution in view of American citizens, political landscape, and world observers.*

Question 8B: *Illustrate the extent of the importance of the Hammurabi's Code in view of today's laws, political landscape, and cultural mores.*

It should be easy to spot the organization for this prompt. The question clearly lists the three topics for you: "citizens, political landscape, and world observers" or "laws, political landscape, and cultural mores." Be sure to answer the question by illustrating the extent in the cause/effect columns and—especially—the conclusion.

Question 9A: *The industrial revolution reshaped America in many ways. Clarify this statement for 1820s America economically, socially, politically.*

Question 9B: *The industrial revolution reshaped Europe in many ways. Clarify this statement for 1700s and 1800s Europe economically, socially, politically.*

It may appear that the three topics are listed for you, and they can be used in this manner, but expanding on their depth may be helpful to answering the question. For example, some possible suggestions are: industrial economy, social change, political directions, political changes, economic opportunities, political hardships, economic ideology, socio-cultural influences, employment economics, political leadership, etc. The choice of how one may employ these potential topics is dependent on the author's familiarity with the content and level of writing sophistication. The 5-Minute Drill provides a plethora of opportunities for writers to be creative and clever with whatever writing tools you possess.

Question 10A: *Evaluate the treatment of African-Americans in the South during the Reconstruction Era. Be sure to include black women, children, and free laborers in your response.*

Question 10B: *Evaluate the treatment of Africans in view of Europeans during the Age of Exploration. Be sure to include African women, children, and free laborers in your response.*

Although the question contains three subcategories, the three listed are not broad enough in most cases to use as topics. Better topics may be "leadership," "political ideologies," and "treatment." The standard "political, economic, and social" would adequately do the job here, again. Nevertheless, be sure the specifics illustrate the treatment of the three African-American subcategories – black women, children, and free laborers. The cause/effect column should just "fall into place" when the thesis is conceptually followed through.

Question 11A: *Biographical literature constitutes a major evolution in a reader's understanding of an era and its peoples. Defend this statement.*

Question 11B: *Biographical literature of the Silk Road constitutes a major evolution in a reader's understanding of the era and its peoples. Defend this statement.*

Having a thesis that tames this type of broad question will assist in developing worthwhile topics, such as: primary source essence, moral growth, experiential maturity, era's attributes, social understanding, cultural desires, proof of progress, advancing education, sharing, etc.

Question 12A: *The NBA's Golden State Warriors are becoming a professional basketball dynasty. Defend or refute this statement.*

Question 12B: *Football, or "soccer" as the American's say it, is becoming the largest international professional sport. Defend or refute this statement.*

With any team concept, topics of success may be: work ethic, talent, understanding the game, coaching/leadership, superior game plan, strength of the league, etc. To refute the question A, topics could appear as: short-lived success, timing, luck, bad officiating, budget imbalance, weak league, etc. For question B, top American sports programs do not include "soccer" for adults. Be sure to defend or refute the statement.

English Literature and Language Applications

The 5-Minute Drill can be used in any course for essay writing and promoting organizational thinking skills. It is true that some modifications may take place to make the 5MD conform to all the unique requirements of specific instructors or courses, but that can be easily done. For example, an exceptional teacher of regular education English courses, as well as AP* English Language and AP* English Literature, has used the 5-Minute Drill for years, mostly for formatting for rhetorical and literary analyses. His experience with working with the College Board® has refined his skills and craft.

Here's what he says about the 5-Minute Drill: "I appreciate its diagnostic aspect; the benefit of having students spend more time on analysis, interpretation, and synthesis (higher level skills on Bloom's taxonomy) rather than on simple regurgitation of facts or summary; the benefit of having the students either do it as an independent assessment or in small groups which inspires student conversation; how it helps struggling students to *see how* to go through the analytical thought process of an argument; how it gives students the ability to assert their own claims and sharpen their thinking; how it gives students an opportunity to evaluate their reasoning and the reasoning of their peers; how it develops confidence in making insightful claims and in avoiding clichés; and how it underscores the students' responsibility to provide evidence and an explanation to support their claims. The 5-Minute Drill helps every writer to improve." What follows are examples of the 5MD variations his students use for rhetorical and literary essays.

Rhetorical Analysis

In the graphic organizer below, make sure that you address all parts of the actual prompt, and adjust the structure of your essay accordingly.

For your conclusion, answer the *So what?* question. How was the author effective in getting her message across by using these rhetorical strategies? For the sake of unity, without repetition, refer back to the beginning of the essay and/or draw a connection between the author's use of rhetorical strategies and her purpose.

Thesis: In (title), (author) action verb (rhetorical strategies) to (author's claim, main idea, or purpose).

Sample Thesis: In his 1962 speech to the nation, President John F. Kennedy used a motivational and urgent tone, patriotic figures of speech, and statistical evidence to put pressure on the steel corporations to lower their prices and to persuade the American people to unite behind him.

Level I	Level II	Level III
Identify author's use of **language** and **rhetorical strategies**	**Provide** textual **evidence** (specifics, quotes, examples from text)	**Explain** why the author uses these strategies, **how** they express the author's ideas, and **what effect** they have on the effectiveness of the essay
A.	1. 2. 3.	1. 2. 3.
B.	1. 2. 3.	1. 2. 3.
C.	1. 2. 3.	1. 2. 3.

Conclusion: How the author effectively communicated his/ her message using these rhetorical strategies.

Literary Analysis

Step 1 – Read and annotate the prompt. **Step 2** – Read and annotate the passage. **Step 3** – Reread the prompt.

Your job: 1) explain the author's meaning, and 2) show how the author does it (particular use of language, literary devices, etc.).

1) Come to an understanding of the author's meaning in its full complexity. Don't simplify it into a cliché that isn't quite right or put words in the author's mouth. Assuming that your reader has read the text and seeks an enlightened interpretation of the passage, make an assertion (the first part of your thesis statement) about the passage that is not obvious, in which you interpret the author's meaning based on evidence you can provide from the text.

2) Then determine **how** the author creates that meaning through language and literary devices (the second part of the thesis statement). **T.A.G.** your thesis statement (write the Title, Author, and Genre of the text). When you write your thesis statement below, state your position confidently as if it were truth; avoid "I think" or "in my opinion"; make sure that all parts of the prompt are addressed; adjust your graphic organizer accordingly. Complete the 5MD graphic organizer below which utilizes **P.I.E.**: Point, Illustration, and Explanation. The main points you fill out to support your thesis should be focused in your topic sentences. Each point or topic must directly support the thesis statement.

T̲itle of text _____

A̲uthor of text _____

G̲enre (poem, play, story, novel) _____

Thesis: In (title), (author) action verb (device) to (your claim, main idea, or purpose).

Sample Thesis: In his poem Sonnet 73, Shakespeare expresses a human life as one rotation of a cycle and death as a reabsorption back into nature by using metaphors of a day, a year, and a fire, by using a first person point of view, and by following the format of a traditional Elizabethan sonnet.

P̲oint	I̲llustration	E̲xplanation
(how?)	(contextual evidence)	(how evidence supports your point & your thesis)
1.		
2.		

Point	Illustration	Explanation

3.

Conclusion: What is the significance of your thesis? Show the value of seeing the ways in which the author used language to create his or her meaning. If possible, you can put it into the context of a literary period or an author's development.

A Letter to Teachers

The 5-Minute Drill is an easy and effective way to organize a structured essay which makes an insightful interpretation and claim, contains evidence to support it, and provides an analytical explanation to answer the most challenging questions. Further, the 5-Minute Drill saves time, gets to the heart of the question's answer, and produces unparalleled success. By the end of the school year, my students' writing skills regularly exceed their reading skills by multiple years because of this simple and quick pre-writing activity. Simply stated, in all my years of teaching, the 5-Minute Drill has positively assisted more students than any other tool.

So often teachers give students the question/prompt and, hopefully, share samples of model essays, but expect students to know (and often struggle through) the complex process of writing the essay. As a result, I developed a writing system called the 5-Minute Drill over a matter of years.

Traditionally, high school students and college freshmen are the ones I teach this system to daily, but third graders have successfully employed its basic elements, so it's great for all levels of writing. You know the system works well when you see the development of high scoring papers with just a few practice efforts; students themselves have even remarked that the 5-Minute Drill is a worthwhile, simple, and clean graphic organizer.

In our classroom, we say in a deep, glottal, sluggish voice, "answer the question." (A bit of vampire-type humor helps everyone to remember the obvious.) With many "answer the question" reminders, students have learned to direct their efforts to fulfill the rubric's version of a quality response by writing an organized essay that clearly answers the question. The "graphic" element of this graphic organizer ensures that the question is answered well and completely.

A surprising benefit of the 5-Minute Drill is its ability to be a wonderful **diagnostic tool** by virtue of allowing students to see incomplete or weak spots in their planning. What needs to be done becomes obvious. Once a writer's weaknesses are diagnosed, tutorials can then begin to assist their development.

Another strength of the 5-Minute Drill is that, with simple modifications, it can accommodate comparison-contrast questions, change-over-time prompts, document-based questions, or any other type of standard essay question. Whether it be the College Board rolling out a new contextualization paragraph or the state requiring an additional viewpoint, the 5-Minute Drill can handle the adjustment. Whether it be a college-level course or an elementary-school "attempt," the 5-Minute Drill maintains its educational integrity.

We all know there are many correct answers to every question; the 5-Minute Drill illustrates this point splendidly. The sharing of papers with peers, a chapter or unit review, and class discussions are assisted greatly with the 5-Minute Drill's divergent possibilities. **This is true learning**— it promotes judging, synthesizing, and evaluating the course content at the highest possible level of thinking.

The 5-Minute Drill helps writers get to the core of the answer, but the transitioning from the 5-Minute Drill to the actual essay does require reasonable essay-writing skills. Not every student can make this transition easily, but most do with just a few practices.

There seems to be a student or two each year that struggles to learn the 5-Minute Drill, and therefore can be apprehensive with the system, even after dozens of attempts. Their efforts to learn the process may be slow, but the 5-Minute Drill still improves their writing skills overall— although, sometimes, not as much as other students. Most students, by far, grasp the process and gain writing and thinking skills during a single school year that would usually only develop over the course of multiple years of growth. The few possible negatives are far outweighed by the numerous positive attributes of the 5-Minute Drill.

From my experience, the best way for students to learn the 5-Minute Drill structure is to

(1) learn/practice the thesis and introductory paragraph separately at an earlier time;

(2) write their first complete 5-Minute Drill with a topic that they know [something about your school, classroom, educational direction, or food works well – see Questions A and B on pages 32 and 34 respectively for samples of this type of practice];

(3) learn by you, the instructor, modeling samples of the 5-Minute Drill multiple times on multiple days [hopefully this will be all it takes for them to learn it, since it is only a common-sense graphic organizer];

(4) write it by themselves, then pair-share, work in a larger group/s, and finally with the instructor's leadership, everyone shares in a whole group;

(5) initially the grading should be on an easy scale [everything is in the right place, the thesis is well done, it makes sense, and it generally answers the question], then the expectations will increase a bit each time;

(6) and finally, once the 5-Minute Drill is understood by the students, they can grade their own 5-Minute Drills to increase the learning curve.

The 5-Minute Drill can most easily be learned through practice.

Author's Acknowledgements

Thanks to the many students who have taught me. In illuminating the gaps in writing/thinking pedagogy, you taught me the elements of the 5 minute drill. Being able to help and guide you young people has been incredibly rewarding.

Thanks to Kurt Fischer for all the invaluable assistance and encouragement, as well as being such a quality educator and person. Your passion for your students and school are more than a blessing to us all. Thank you to all those who helped shape me as a professional and human being: Fred and Helen Mayorga (Mom and Dad), Jim and Betty Witner, Judy Gates, Jim Heintz, Dwight Rees, Raul Nido, Ana Danehy, the Track team, the Pine Canyon Camp family, Anthony Avila, DJ Dance Instructors (Ana, Ama, Elizabeth, Alondra, Rebekah, Mirna and Fernanda), the Sunnyside High School staff, David Nazarian with Sherpa Learning, and ALL the students I have been lucky enough to share time with.

A special thanks to my family; I could not have done any of this without your love and support. To my wife, Kathy, thanks for putting up with my unending commitments. Your boundless passion and quality heart is a true treasure.

Olivia – our love for you is everlasting. Further, our doggies make life so much better.

I cannot imagine life without teaching. What a gift it is to share stories, knowledge, GOOD humor, skills, goals, morals, camp, smiles, food (and lots of it!), homework, successes, current events, and life-building foundations with all of the wonderful people that God has given us the opportunity to share time with during our short ride on this planet.

Let's continue to give back (Romans 12:2) and make the world a better place.

About the Author

RICH MAYORGA has been a student advocate and educator for over 35 years, and was Arizona's Teacher of the Year in 2003. He has been teaching AP U.S. History at Sunnyside High School in Tucson for 23 years, and is also a nine year veteran adjunct professor at Pima Community College. For a 12 year period, Rich taught four AP courses (AP World, AP U.S., AP Gov., and AP Econ.) *concurrently.* Rich's exceptional efforts in the classroom have earned him dozens of awards and got him inducted into the Sunnyside USD's Hall of Fame in 2005.

Rich earned his BA, MA, and Ed.S. (Educational Specialist) degrees from the University of AZ, and in 2003 was presented with an honorary Doctorates Degree of Humane Letters from Northern Arizona University. Since 2000, Rich has worked closely with the College Board, serving on the Academic Advisory Council (AAC) and as a Reader, Table Leader, and Exam Leader for the AP US History national exam. From 2006-2009, he was one of two high school teachers selected nationally to serve on the SAT II – US History Committee, and in 2007, to publish sample curriculum in the College Board's *AP U.S. History Teacher's Guide.* In 2004, he was selected by the AZ Dept.

of Education to present a lesson on Progressivism and the 5-Minute Drill for the state's Best Practices Video Cases project.*

For the last 3 decades, Rich has worked regularly as a director at Christian camps for impoverished youth. He is also a philanthropic DJ, donating all proceeds to a variety of causes. Rich served in the U.S. Marine Corps for four years. An admitted workaholic, Rich still makes his faith and family his priorities and finds time to go for a run each and every day.

* To view or download the video lesson, "Theodore Roosevelt and Progessivisim," go to http://pt3.nau.edu/media/mayorga.mov

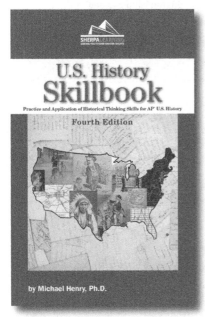